PRIORITIES

TO DO

NOTES:

PRIORITIES

TO DO

NOTES:

PRIORITIES

TO DO

NOTES:

PRIORITIES

TO DO

NOTES:

PRIORITIES

TO DO

NOTES:

PRIORITIES

TO DO

NOTES:

PRIORITIES

TO DO

NOTES:

PRIORITIES

TO DO

NOTES:

PRIORITIES

TO DO

NOTES:

PRIORITIES

TO DO

NOTES:

PRIORITIES

TO DO

NOTES:

PRIORITIES

TO DO

NOTES:

PRIORITIES

TO DO

NOTES:

PRIORITIES

TO DO

NOTES:

PRIORITIES

TO DO

NOTES:

PRIORITIES

TO DO

NOTES:

PRIORITIES

TO DO

NOTES:

PRIORITIES

TO DO

NOTES:

PRIORITIES

TO DO

NOTES:

PRIORITIES

TO DO

NOTES:

PRIORITIES

_____

_____

_____

_____

_____

_____

TO DO

_____

_____

_____

_____

_____

_____

_____

_____

_____

NOTES:

PRIORITIES

TO DO

NOTES:

PRIORITIES

TO DO

NOTES:

PRIORITIES

TO DO

NOTES:

PRIORITIES

TO DO

NOTES:

PRIORITIES

TO DO

NOTES:

PRIORITIES

TO DO

NOTES:

PRIORITIES

TO DO

NOTES:

PRIORITIES

TO DO

NOTES:

PRIORITIES

TO DO

NOTES:

PRIORITIES

TO DO

NOTES:

PRIORITIES

TO DO

NOTES:

PRIORITIES

TO DO

NOTES:

PRIORITIES

TO DO

NOTES:

PRIORITIES

TO DO

NOTES:

PRIORITIES

TO DO

NOTES:

PRIORITIES

TO DO

NOTES:

PRIORITIES

TO DO

NOTES:

PRIORITIES

TO DO

NOTES:

PRIORITIES

_____

_____

_____

_____

_____

TO DO

_____

_____

_____

_____

_____

_____

_____

_____

_____

_____

_____

NOTES:

PRIORITIES

TO DO

NOTES:

PRIORITIES

TO DO

NOTES:

PRIORITIES

TO DO

NOTES:

PRIORITIES

TO DO

NOTES:

PRIORITIES

TO DO

NOTES:

PRIORITIES

TO DO

NOTES:

PRIORITIES

TO DO

NOTES:

PRIORITIES

TO DO

NOTES:

PRIORITIES

TO DO

NOTES:

PRIORITIES

TO DO

NOTES:

PRIORITIES

TO DO

NOTES:

PRIORITIES

TO DO

NOTES:

PRIORITIES

TO DO

NOTES:

PRIORITIES

TO DO

NOTES:

PRIORITIES

TO DO

NOTES:

PRIORITIES

TO DO

NOTES:

PRIORITIES

TO DO

NOTES:

PRIORITIES

TO DO

NOTES:

PRIORITIES

TO DO

NOTES:

PRIORITIES

TO DO

NOTES:

PRIORITIES

TO DO

NOTES:

PRIORITIES

TO DO

NOTES:

PRIORITIES

TO DO

NOTES:

PRIORITIES

TO DO

NOTES:

PRIORITIES

TO DO

NOTES:

PRIORITIES

TO DO

NOTES:

PRIORITIES

TO DO

NOTES:

PRIORITIES

TO DO

NOTES:

PRIORITIES

TO DO

NOTES:

PRIORITIES

TO DO

NOTES:

PRIORITIES

TO DO

NOTES:

PRIORITIES

TO DO

NOTES:

PRIORITIES

TO DO

NOTES:

PRIORITIES

TO DO

NOTES:

PRIORITIES

TO DO

NOTES:

PRIORITIES

TO DO

NOTES:

PRIORITIES

TO DO

NOTES:

PRIORITIES

TO DO

NOTES:

PRIORITIES

TO DO

NOTES:

PRIORITIES

TO DO

NOTES:

PRIORITIES

TO DO

NOTES:

PRIORITIES

TO DO

NOTES:

PRIORITIES

TO DO

NOTES:

PRIORITIES

TO DO

NOTES:

PRIORITIES

TO DO

NOTES:

PRIORITIES

TO DO

NOTES:

PRIORITIES

TO DO

NOTES:

PRIORITIES

TO DO

NOTES:

PRIORITIES

TO DO

NOTES:

PRIORITIES

TO DO

NOTES:

PRIORITIES

TO DO

NOTES:

PRIORITIES

TO DO

NOTES:

PRIORITIES

TO DO

NOTES:

PRIORITIES

TO DO

NOTES:

PRIORITIES

TO DO

NOTES:

PRIORITIES

TO DO

NOTES:

PRIORITIES

TO DO

NOTES:

PRIORITIES

TO DO

NOTES:

PRIORITIES

TO DO

NOTES:

PRIORITIES

TO DO

NOTES:

PRIORITIES

TO DO

NOTES:

PRIORITIES

TO DO

NOTES:

PRIORITIES

TO DO

NOTES:

PRIORITIES

TO DO

NOTES:

PRIORITIES

TO DO

NOTES:

PRIORITIES

TO DO

NOTES:

PRIORITIES

TO DO

NOTES:

PRIORITIES

_____

_____

_____

_____

_____

_____

TO DO

_____

_____

_____

_____

_____

_____

_____

_____

_____

_____

_____

NOTES:

PRIORITIES

TO DO

NOTES:

PRIORITIES

TO DO

NOTES:

PRIORITIES

TO DO

NOTES:

PRIORITIES

TO DO

NOTES:

PRIORITIES

TO DO

NOTES:

PRIORITIES

TO DO

NOTES:

PRIORITIES

TO DO

NOTES:

PRIORITIES

TO DO

NOTES:

PRIORITIES

TO DO

NOTES:

PRIORITIES

TO DO

NOTES:

PRIORITIES

TO DO

NOTES:

PRIORITIES

TO DO

NOTES:

PRIORITIES

TO DO

NOTES:

PRIORITIES

TO DO

NOTES:

PRIORITIES

TO DO

NOTES:

PRIORITIES

TO DO

NOTES:

PRIORITIES

TO DO

NOTES:

PRIORITIES

TO DO

NOTES:

PRIORITIES

TO DO

NOTES:

PRIORITIES

TO DO

NOTES:

PRIORITIES

TO DO

NOTES:

PRIORITIES

TO DO

NOTES:

PRIORITIES

TO DO

NOTES:

PRIORITIES

TO DO

NOTES:

PRIORITIES

TO DO

NOTES:

PRIORITIES

TO DO

NOTES:

PRIORITIES

TO DO

NOTES:

PRIORITIES

TO DO

NOTES:

PRIORITIES

TO DO

NOTES:

PRIORITIES

TO DO

NOTES:

PRIORITIES

TO DO

NOTES:

PRIORITIES

_____

_____

_____

_____

_____

_____

TO DO

_____

_____

_____

_____

_____

_____

_____

_____

_____

_____

_____

_____

_____

NOTES:

_____

_____

_____

_____

_____

PRIORITIES

TO DO

NOTES:

PRIORITIES

TO DO

NOTES:

PRIORITIES

TO DO

NOTES:

PRIORITIES

TO DO

NOTES:

PRIORITIES

TO DO

NOTES:

PRIORITIES

TO DO

NOTES:

PRIORITIES

TO DO

NOTES:

PRIORITIES

TO DO

NOTES:

PRIORITIES

TO DO

NOTES:

PRIORITIES

TO DO

NOTES:

PRIORITIES

TO DO

NOTES:

PRIORITIES

TO DO

NOTES:

PRIORITIES

TO DO

NOTES:

PRIORITIES

TO DO

NOTES:

PRIORITIES

TO DO

NOTES:

PRIORITIES

TO DO

NOTES:

PRIORITIES

TO DO

NOTES:

PRIORITIES

TO DO

NOTES:

PRIORITIES

TO DO

NOTES:

PRIORITIES

TO DO

NOTES:

PRIORITIES

TO DO

NOTES:

PRIORITIES

TO DO

NOTES:

PRIORITIES

TO DO

NOTES:

PRIORITIES

TO DO

NOTES:

PRIORITIES

TO DO

NOTES:

PRIORITIES

TO DO

NOTES:

PRIORITIES

TO DO

NOTES:

PRIORITIES

TO DO

NOTES:

PRIORITIES

TO DO

NOTES:

PRIORITIES

TO DO

NOTES:

PRIORITIES

TO DO

NOTES:

PRIORITIES

TO DO

NOTES:

PRIORITIES

TO DO

NOTES:

PRIORITIES

TO DO

NOTES:

PRIORITIES

TO DO

NOTES:

PRIORITIES

TO DO

NOTES:

PRIORITIES

TO DO

NOTES:

PRIORITIES

TO DO

NOTES:

PRIORITIES

TO DO

NOTES:

PRIORITIES

TO DO

NOTES:

PRIORITIES

TO DO

NOTES:

PRIORITIES

TO DO

NOTES:

PRIORITIES

TO DO

NOTES:

PRIORITIES

TO DO

NOTES:

PRIORITIES

TO DO

NOTES:

PRIORITIES

TO DO

NOTES:

PRIORITIES

TO DO

NOTES:

PRIORITIES

TO DO

NOTES:

PRIORITIES

TO DO

NOTES:

PRIORITIES

TO DO

NOTES:

PRIORITIES

TO DO

NOTES:

PRIORITIES

TO DO

NOTES:

PRIORITIES

TO DO

NOTES:

PRIORITIES

TO DO

NOTES:

PRIORITIES

TO DO

NOTES:

PRIORITIES

TO DO

NOTES:

PRIORITIES

TO DO

NOTES:

PRIORITIES

TO DO

NOTES:

PRIORITIES

TO DO

NOTES:

PRIORITIES

TO DO

NOTES:

PRIORITIES

TO DO

NOTES:

PRIORITIES

TO DO

NOTES:

PRIORITIES

TO DO

NOTES:

PRIORITIES

TO DO

NOTES:

PRIORITIES

TO DO

NOTES:

PRIORITIES

TO DO

NOTES:

PRIORITIES

TO DO

NOTES:

PRIORITIES

TO DO

NOTES:

PRIORITIES

TO DO

NOTES:

PRIORITIES

TO DO

NOTES:

PRIORITIES

TO DO

NOTES:

PRIORITIES

TO DO

NOTES:

PRIORITIES

TO DO

NOTES:

PRIORITIES

TO DO

NOTES:

PRIORITIES

TO DO

NOTES:

PRIORITIES

TO DO

NOTES:

PRIORITIES

TO DO

NOTES:

PRIORITIES

TO DO

NOTES:

PRIORITIES

TO DO

NOTES:

PRIORITIES

TO DO

NOTES:

PRIORITIES

TO DO

NOTES:

PRIORITIES

TO DO

NOTES:

PRIORITIES

TO DO

NOTES:

PRIORITIES

TO DO

NOTES:

PRIORITIES

TO DO

NOTES:

PRIORITIES

TO DO

NOTES:

PRIORITIES

TO DO

NOTES:

PRIORITIES

TO DO

NOTES:

PRIORITIES

TO DO

NOTES:

PRIORITIES

_____

_____

_____

_____

_____

_____

TO DO

_____

_____

_____

_____

_____

_____

_____

_____

_____

_____

_____

_____

NOTES:

PRIORITIES

TO DO

NOTES:

PRIORITIES

TO DO

NOTES:

PRIORITIES

TO DO

NOTES:

PRIORITIES

TO DO

NOTES:

PRIORITIES

TO DO

NOTES:

PRIORITIES

TO DO

NOTES:

PRIORITIES

TO DO

NOTES:

PRIORITIES

TO DO

NOTES:

PRIORITIES

TO DO

NOTES:

PRIORITIES

TO DO

NOTES:

PRIORITIES

TO DO

NOTES:

PRIORITIES

TO DO

NOTES:

PRIORITIES

TO DO

NOTES:

TO DO

NOTES:

PRIORITIES

TO DO

NOTES:

TO DO

NOTES:

PRIORITIES

TO DO

NOTES:

PRIORITIES

TO DO

NOTES:

PRIORITIES

TO DO

NOTES:

PRIORITIES

TO DO

NOTES:

PRIORITIES

TO DO

NOTES:

PRIORITIES

TO DO

NOTES:

PRIORITIES

TO DO

NOTES:

PRIORITIES

TO DO

NOTES:

PRIORITIES

TO DO

NOTES:

PRIORITIES

TO DO

NOTES:

PRIORITIES

TO DO

NOTES:

PRIORITIES

TO DO

NOTES:

PRIORITIES

TO DO

NOTES:

PRIORITIES

TO DO

NOTES:

PRIORITIES

TO DO

NOTES:

PRIORITIES

TO DO

NOTES:

PRIORITIES

TO DO

NOTES:

PRIORITIES

TO DO

NOTES:

PRIORITIES

TO DO

NOTES:

PRIORITIES

TO DO

NOTES:

PRIORITIES

TO DO

NOTES:

PRIORITIES

TO DO

NOTES:

PRIORITIES

TO DO

NOTES:

PRIORITIES

TO DO

NOTES:

PRIORITIES

TO DO

NOTES:

PRIORITIES

_____
_____
_____
_____
_____
_____

TO DO

_____
_____
_____
_____
_____
_____
_____
_____
_____
_____
_____
_____

NOTES:

PRIORITIES

TO DO

NOTES:

PRIORITIES

TO DO

NOTES:

PRIORITIES

TO DO

NOTES:

PRIORITIES

TO DO

NOTES:

PRIORITIES

TO DO

NOTES:

PRIORITIES

TO DO

NOTES:

PRIORITIES

TO DO

NOTES:

PRIORITIES

TO DO

NOTES:

PRIORITIES

TO DO

NOTES:

PRIORITIES

TO DO

NOTES:

PRIORITIES

TO DO

NOTES:

PRIORITIES

TO DO

NOTES:

PRIORITIES

TO DO

NOTES:

PRIORITIES

TO DO

NOTES:

PRIORITIES

TO DO

NOTES:

PRIORITIES

TO DO

NOTES:

PRIORITIES

TO DO

NOTES:

PRIORITIES

TO DO

NOTES:

PRIORITIES

TO DO

NOTES:

PRIORITIES

TO DO

NOTES:

PRIORITIES

TO DO

NOTES:

PRIORITIES

TO DO

NOTES:

PRIORITIES

TO DO

NOTES:

PRIORITIES

TO DO

NOTES:

PRIORITIES

TO DO

NOTES:

PRIORITIES

TO DO

NOTES:

PRIORITIES

TO DO

NOTES:

PRIORITIES

TO DO

NOTES:

PRIORITIES

TO DO

NOTES:

PRIORITIES

TO DO

NOTES:

PRIORITIES

TO DO

NOTES:

PRIORITIES

TO DO

NOTES:

PRIORITIES

TO DO

NOTES:

PRIORITIES

TO DO

NOTES:

PRIORITIES

TO DO

NOTES:

PRIORITIES

TO DO

NOTES:

PRIORITIES

TO DO

NOTES:

PRIORITIES

TO DO

NOTES:

PRIORITIES

TO DO

NOTES:

PRIORITIES

TO DO

NOTES:

PRIORITIES

TO DO

NOTES:

PRIORITIES

TO DO

NOTES:

PRIORITIES

TO DO

NOTES:

PRIORITIES

TO DO

NOTES:

PRIORITIES

TO DO

NOTES:

PRIORITIES

TO DO

NOTES:

PRIORITIES

TO DO

NOTES:

PRIORITIES

TO DO

NOTES:

PRIORITIES

TO DO

NOTES:

PRIORITIES

TO DO

NOTES:

PRIORITIES

TO DO

NOTES:

PRIORITIES

TO DO

NOTES:

PRIORITIES

TO DO

NOTES:

PRIORITIES

TO DO

NOTES:

PRIORITIES

TO DO

NOTES:

PRIORITIES

TO DO

NOTES:

PRIORITIES

TO DO

NOTES:

PRIORITIES

TO DO

NOTES:

PRIORITIES

TO DO

NOTES:

PRIORITIES

TO DO

NOTES:

PRIORITIES

TO DO

NOTES:

PRIORITIES

TO DO

NOTES:

PRIORITIES

TO DO

NOTES:

PRIORITIES

TO DO

NOTES:

PRIORITIES

TO DO

NOTES:

PRIORITIES

TO DO

NOTES:

PRIORITIES

TO DO

NOTES:

PRIORITIES

TO DO

NOTES:

PRIORITIES

TO DO

NOTES:

PRIORITIES

●

TO DO

NOTES:

PRIORITIES

TO DO

NOTES:

PRIORITIES

TO DO

NOTES:

PRIORITIES

TO DO

NOTES:

PRIORITIES

TO DO

NOTES:

PRIORITIES

TO DO

NOTES:

PRIORITIES

TO DO

NOTES:

PRIORITIES

TO DO

NOTES:

PRIORITIES

TO DO

NOTES:

PRIORITIES

TO DO

NOTES:

PRIORITIES

TO DO

NOTES:

PRIORITIES

TO DO

NOTES:

PRIORITIES

TO DO

NOTES:

PRIORITIES

TO DO

NOTES:

PRIORITIES

TO DO

NOTES:

PRIORITIES

TO DO

NOTES:

PRIORITIES

TO DO

NOTES:

PRIORITIES

TO DO

NOTES:

PRIORITIES

TO DO

NOTES:

PRIORITIES

TO DO

NOTES:

PRIORITIES

TO DO

NOTES:

PRIORITIES

TO DO

NOTES:

PRIORITIES

TO DO

NOTES:

PRIORITIES

TO DO

NOTES: